Presidents
Activity Book

Tony J. Tallarico

total:
___

Dover Publications, Inc.
Mineola, New York

Bibliographical Note

Presidents Activity Book is a new work, first published by
Dover Publications, Inc., in 2009.

International Standard Book Number
ISBN-13: 978-0-486-47388-8
ISBN-10: 0-486-47388-0

Manufactured in the United States by RR Donnelley
47388004   2015
www.doverpublications.com

Note

This little book is filled with fun activities, and each one features one of the presidents of the United States. From George Washington to Barack Obama, you can complete word searches, spot-the-differences, mazes, and more—you can even use special decoder charts to decipher fun facts! Do you know which President's birthday fell on Independence Day? Or which one loved jellybeans? Find out what Ronald Reagan's job was before he became president, and what musical instrument Harry S. Truman played. You'll even learn about the special duties of the president, interesting facts about the White House and other monuments, as well as exciting events in U.S. history. Do your best to solve each puzzle, but if you get stuck, there is a Solutions section that begins on page 53.

Barack H. Obama is our country's first African-American President. Although Obama is the 44th U.S. President, there have actually been just 43. How is that possible?

	1	2	3	4	5	6	7
A	V	N	H	I	T	O	J
B	A	G	F	E	C	I	S
C	L	D	R	W	U	B	K

— — — — — —   — — — — — — — — —
B2 C3 A6 A1 B4 C3   B5 C1 B4 A1 B4 C1 B1 A2 C2

H E L D   O F F I C E

— — — — — — ,   — — —   — — —
A5 C4 B6 B5 B4   C6 C5 A5   A2 A6 A5

G R O V E R ,   C L E V E L A N D

— — —   — — —   — — —   — — —
A4 A2   B1   C3 A6 C4   A3 B4   C4 B1 B7

T H E   2 2 N D   A N D

— — — — — —   — — —
C1 B1 A5 B4 C3   A5 A3 B4

2 4 T H   P R E S I D E N T .

Each letter-number combination represents a letter. Use the chart above to fill in the blanks and decode the answer.

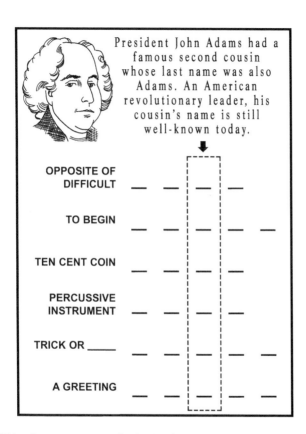

President John Adams had a famous second cousin whose last name was also Adams. An American revolutionary leader, his cousin's name is still well-known today.

OPPOSITE OF DIFFICULT _ _ _ _

TO BEGIN _ _ _ _ _

TEN CENT COIN _ _ _ _

PERCUSSIVE INSTRUMENT _ _ _ _

TRICK OR ____ _ _ _ _ _

A GREETING _ _ _ _ _

Write the answer to each clue in the spaces provided, and his cousin's first name will appear in the box.

5

Which U.S. territory became a state during
Andrew Jackson's presidency
(between 1829 - 1837)?

A	W	E	R	D	N	A
J	A	C	K	S	O	N
A	N	D	R	E	W	D
C	D	R		K	E	R
K	R	A		N	R	E
S	E	S	A	S	D	W
O	W	E	R	D	N	A
N	O	S	K	C	A	J

— — — — — — — — —

The name ANDREW appears 6 times in the word search and
JACKSON appears 3 times. Find and circle them all. Then
write the remaining letters on the spaces provided.

6

Three U.S. Presidents died on July 4 (John Adams & Thomas Jefferson in 1826 and James Monroe in 1831) but only one was born on Independence Day.

☆ C	✿ E	☆ A	☆ L	❖ E	◯ N	☆ V
☐ A	☆ I	☆ N	☆ C	☆ O	☆ O	✿ U
☆ L	☆ I	◯ S	☆ D	☆ G	☆ E	◯ N
☆ O	☆ U	☆ R	☐ 2	☆ 3	☆ 0	☆ T
☐ E	☆ H	◯ 4	☆ P	❖ E	☆ R	☆ E
☆ S	☆ I	☆ D	✿ A	☆ E	☆ N	☆ T
☆ I	☆ N	☆ 1	❖ 7	☆ 8	☆ 7	☆ 2

To find out his name, circle all the letters and numbers with a ☆ above them. Write them in the order that they appear in the spaces provided.

James Buchanan, our 15th U.S. President,
was the only president who never had a wife.
Who served as White House hostess?

To find the answer, use a dark-colored pencil or crayon to fill
in all the spaces that contain a ☆.

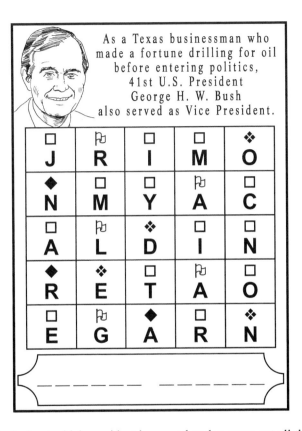

As a Texas businessman who made a fortune drilling for oil before entering politics, 41st U.S. President George H. W. Bush also served as Vice President.

□ J	ᛒ R	□ I	□ M	❖ O
◆ N	□ M	□ Y	ᛒ A	□ C
□ A	ᛒ L	❖ D	□ I	□ N
◆ R	❖ E	□ T	ᛒ A	□ O
□ E	ᛒ G	◆ A	□ R	❖ N

_ _ _ _ _   _ _ _ _ _

To find out which president he served under, cross out all the letters that have a □ above them. Then write the remaining letters in the order that they appear on the spaces provided.

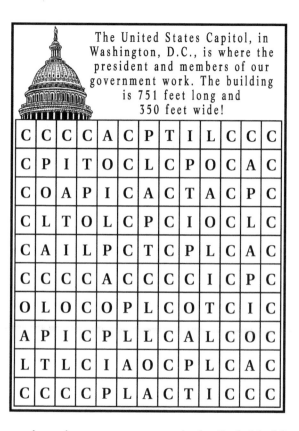

The United States Capitol, in Washington, D.C., is where the president and members of our government work. The building is 751 feet long and 350 feet wide!

C	C	C	A	C	P	T	I	L	C	C	C
C	P	I	T	O	C	L	C	P	O	C	A	C
C	O	A	P	I	C	A	C	T	A	C	P	C
C	L	T	O	L	C	P	C	I	O	C	L	C
C	A	I	L	P	C	T	C	P	L	C	A	C
C	C	C	C	A	C	C	C	C	I	C	P	C
O	L	O	C	O	P	L	C	O	T	C	I	C
A	P	I	C	P	L	L	C	A	L	C	O	C
L	T	L	C	I	A	O	C	P	L	C	A	C
C	C	C	C	P	L	A	C	T	I	C	C	C

Do you know how many rooms are in the Capitol building? Color all the boxes that contain a **C** to find out.

10

This president was the first to have a Christmas tree in the White House.

| BEFORE | __ __ T __ __ |
| | 3   1   14   12 |

BEFORE __ __ **T** __ __
      3   1   14   12

FAKE __ __ **A** __
    2   11   6

CRUEL __ __ __ **D**
     5   10   4

CLOSE **O** __ **E** __
          9   8

ADULT __ **H** __ **L** **D**
     13   7

__ __ __ __ __ __ __ __
1   2   3   4   5   6   7   8

__ __ __ __ __ __
9   10   11   12   13   14

To find the answer, write the opposite of each word in the spaces provided next to it. Then use the numbers under each blank at the bottom of the page to fill in the correct letters.

11

Bill Clinton, born August 19,
1946 in Hope, Arkansas, was
our 42nd U.S. President.
A saxophone player, he
once considered becoming
a professional musician.

✗	✶	✗	✗	✗	♣	✗	✗	✗	◉	✗	✗	✗
✗	♣	✗	✶	✗	✶	✗	♣	✗	✶	✗	✗	✗
✗	◉	✗	♣	✗	✶	✗	✶	✗	◇	◉	♣	✗
✗	✶	✗	✗	✗	◉	✗	✗	✗	✶	✶	◇	✗
✗	✶	♣	◇	✗	✶	✶	♣	✗	◉	✗	✗	✗
✗	✶	♣	◉	✗	♣	◇	◉	✗	♣	✗	✗	✗
✗	◉	✶	✶	✗	✶	○	□	✗	✶	◉	✶	✗
✗	◇	♣	□	✗	◇	♣	✶	✗	◇	♣	✶	✗
✗	✶	✶	◉	✗	✶	◉	◇	✗	○	✗	✗	✗
✗	◇	□	✶	✗	◇	✶	♣	✗	✶	✗	✗	✗

Color in all the squares containing an ✗ to find out what year
President Clinton took office.

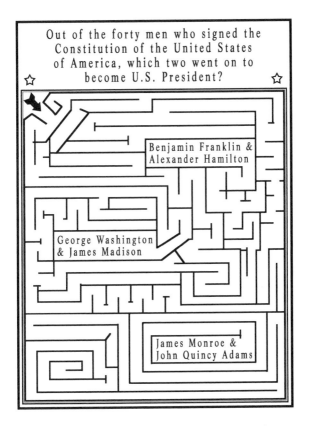

Out of the forty men who signed the Constitution of the United States of America, which two went on to become U.S. President?

Benjamin Franklin & Alexander Hamilton

George Washington & James Madison

James Monroe & John Quincy Adams

Without crossing over any lines, follow the path to the correct answer. Begin at the arrow.

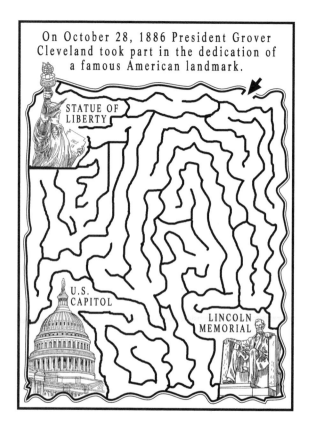

On October 28, 1886 President Grover Cleveland took part in the dedication of a famous American landmark.

STATUE OF LIBERTY

U.S. CAPITOL

LINCOLN MEMORIAL

To find out which landmark it was, follow the path without crossing over any lines. Begin at the arrow.

Dwight D. Eisenhower, our 34th President was nicknamed "Ike." Prior to becoming president in 1953, he was a Five Star General during World War Two.

Can you find and circle the two pictures of General Eisenhower that are exactly the same?

In 1910, this man was the first U.S. President to throw out the first ball of the baseball season. (Nearly all U.S.Presidents since him have followed the tradition!)

BATTER • CATCH • PITCHER
RUNNER • TEAMS • THROW

B	W	I	L	L	T	R
A	I	A	M	H	E	E
T	H	O	R	W	A	H
T	A	O	R	D	M	C
E	W	T	A	F	S	T
R	U	N	N	E	R	I
T	H	C	T	A	C	P

_ _ _ _ _ _ _

_ _ _ _ _ _   _ _ _ _

First, find and circle the baseball words in the word search. Then list the remaining letters in the order that they appear in the blank spaces provided.

16

He was the first U.S. President to be born an American citizen. The first 7 U.S. Presidents were born before the U.S. became its own country.

MNAAYLR (Baltimore is its largest city)	⃝⃝⃝ _ _ _ _ D
ETSA (The Lone Star State)	⃝ _ X _ _
SLLINIO (Springfield is the capital)	I _ ⃝⃝ _ _ _
NOVEMT (Leading producer of maple syrup)	⃝ _ R _ _ _ _
RIAAON (The capital city is Phoenix)	⃝ _ _ Z _ ⃝
EBNRSAK (Omaha is its largest city)	_ _ ⃝ _ _ _ _ A
RIUOSIS (The Show-Me State)	M _ _ _ _ ⃝⃝ _
NOROE (Portland is the largest city)	_ _ ⃝ G _ ⃝

_ _ _ _ _ _ _ _ _ _ _ _

Use the clues to help you unscramble the names of these U.S. states. Write the correct answer in the spaces provided. Then, write the circled letters in the order that they appear in the blanks at the bottom of the page.

17

Who was the first U.S. President to be born in a hospital?

31ST PRESIDENT
HERBERT HOOVER

36TH PRESIDENT
LYNDON B. JOHNSON

39TH PRESIDENT
JIMMY CARTER

To find the answer, use a dark pencil or crayon to color in all the spaces that contain a ●.

He was chosen to replace the vice president in 1973 and later became our nation's leader when the previous president quit - making him the only U.S. President never to run for office.

GLAD	L _ D	_
EASY	_ A Y	_
RENT	T _ N	_
HAUNT	H U _ T	_
WORLD	W _ R D	_
DRAW	R _ W	_
FOUR	O U _	_
OPEN	_ E N	_
RACE	A C _	_
DRINK	R I _ K	_

To learn his name, use one letter from the word in the first column to spell out a word in the second. Write the letter you did not use in the third column. The letters in the third column will spell out the name.

The Founding Fathers of the United States
are those who took part in the American
Revolution and the birth of our nation.
Which U.S. President is credited with
coining the phrase "Founding Fathers?"

ADAMS
BRAXTON
FLOYD
FRANKLIN
HALL
HART
JEFFERSON
LEWIS
PACA
PAINE
PENN
READ
ROSS

N	I	L	K	N	A	R	F
O	H	W	A	D	C	R	H
S	A	R	Y	E	A	N	A
R	L	O	G	H	P	A	R
E	L	R	D	A	E	R	T
F	N	O	T	X	A	R	B
F	S	I	W	E	L	O	D
E	A	D	A	M	S	S	I
J	N	N	E	P	N	S	G

__ __ __ __ __ __ __ .

__ __ __ __ __ __

To find out, circle the names of the founding fathers in the
word search. Then, write the letters that remain in the order
that they appear on the spaces provided.

They are the only grandparent-grandchild pair of U.S. Presidents.

A=14 B=7 D=12 E=1 H=4 I=15 J=2 L=9
M=6 N=11 O=3 R=8 S=13 W=5 Y=10

$\overline{5}$ $\overline{15}$ $\overline{9}$ $\overline{9}$ $\overline{15}$ $\overline{14}$ $\overline{6}$

$\overline{4}$ $\overline{1}$ $\overline{11}$ $\overline{8}$ $\overline{10}$

$\overline{4}$ $\overline{14}$ $\overline{8}$ $\overline{8}$ $\overline{15}$ $\overline{13}$ $\overline{3}$ $\overline{11}$

$\overline{14}$ $\overline{11}$ $\overline{12}$

$\overline{7}$ $\overline{1}$ $\overline{11}$ $\overline{2}$ $\overline{14}$ $\overline{6}$ $\overline{15}$ $\overline{11}$

$\overline{4}$ $\overline{14}$ $\overline{8}$ $\overline{8}$ $\overline{15}$ $\overline{13}$ $\overline{3}$ $\overline{11}$

Use the chart to decode their names.

Ulysses S. Grant was our 18th U.S. President.

He served as a general in the Union army during the Civil War.

Can you find and circle 8 things in the picture on the bottom that make it different from the one on top?

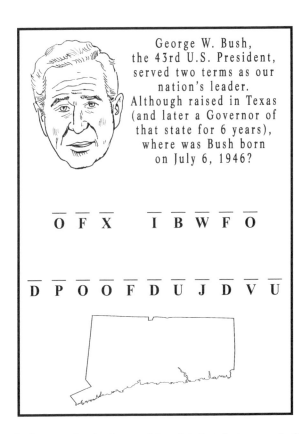

George W. Bush, the 43rd U.S. President, served two terms as our nation's leader. Although raised in Texas (and later a Governor of that state for 6 years), where was Bush born on July 6, 1946?

$\overline{}$ $\overline{O}$ $\overline{F}$ $\overline{X}$ $\overline{I}$ $\overline{B}$ $\overline{W}$ $\overline{F}$ $\overline{O}$

$\overline{D}$ $\overline{P}$ $\overline{O}$ $\overline{O}$ $\overline{F}$ $\overline{D}$ $\overline{U}$ $\overline{J}$ $\overline{D}$ $\overline{V}$ $\overline{U}$

To find out, write the letter of the alphabet that comes **before** each of the letters on the space above it.

Which annual holiday tradition began during Rutherford B. Hayes' term as our 19th U.S. President?

DISPLAY
H S W O $\overline{6}\ \overline{2}\ \overline{12}\ \overline{1}$

SIP
K N I D R $\underline{\quad}\ \overline{9}\ \overline{3}\ \underline{\quad}\ \underline{\quad}$

DIVIDE
S E T P A R A E $\underline{\quad}\ \overline{5}\ \underline{\quad}\ \overline{8}\ \overline{11}\ \underline{\quad}\ \overline{4}\ \overline{7}$

LARGE
G I B $\underline{\quad}\ \underline{\quad}\ \overline{10}$

$\overline{1}\ \overline{2}\ \overline{3}\ \overline{4}\ \overline{5}$ H O U $\underline{\quad}$ E
                         $\overline{6}$

$\overline{7}\ \overline{8}$ S T E $\overline{9}$

E $\overline{10}$ G $\overline{11}\ \overline{12}$ L L

Use the clues provided to unscramble each word, and write it on the blank spaces provided. Then write the numbered letters in the correct spaces on the bottom of this page.

24

Before serving as president, Andrew Jackson was a colonel during the War of 1812.

The letter **J** is hidden in this picture of President Jackson 10 times. Find and circle them all.

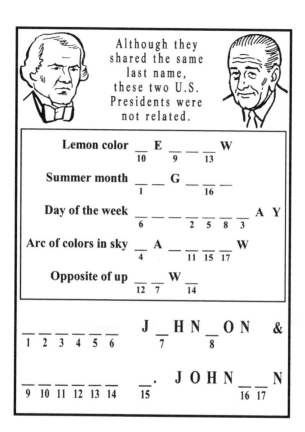

Although they shared the same last name, these two U.S. Presidents were not related.

Lemon color _ E _ _ W
         10 9   13

Summer month _ _ G _ _ _
            1   16

Day of the week _ _ _ _ _ _ _ A Y
             6   2 5 8 3

Arc of colors in sky _ A _ _ _ _ W
              4   11 15 17

Opposite of up _ _ W _
            12 7   14

_ _ _ _ _ _   J _ H N _ O N   &
1 2 3 4 5 6   7   8

_ _ _ _ _ _   _. J O H N _ _ N
9 10 11 12 13 14 15   16 17

Use the clues to solve each puzzle and write the answer in the blank spaces provided. Then write the numbered letters in the correct spaces on the bottom of this page.

26

John F. Kennedy, our 35th President, was born on May 29, 1917. This made him the first U.S. President to be born in the

_____ .

	YES	NO
SHOES ARE WORN ON THE FEET	2	1
DOGS CAN READ BOOKS	3	0
MARBLES ARE SQUARE	H	T
A DIME EQUALS FIVE CENTS	T	H
A BABY CAT IS A KITTEN	C	D
JUNE IS THE SIXTH MONTH	E	A
CARS RUN ON MILK	M	N
BIRDS CAN FLY	T	O
A UNICYCLE HAS FIVE WHEELS	S	U
TEXAS IS A COUNTRY	E	R
SNOW IS COLD	Y	S

To finish this fun fact, first read each sentence, then circle the number or letter in the **YES** column if it's true, or the **NO** column if it's false. Read the circled letters from top to bottom.

Abraham Lincoln, our 16th U.S.
President, was the first
president born outside of the
original thirteen colonies.

↓

QUEEN'S HUSBAND ___ ___ ___ ___

OPPOSITE OF EAST ___ ___ ___ ___

FIVE PLUS FOUR ___ ___ ___

SMALL ROCK ___ ___ ___ ___ ___

EIGHT OUNCES ___ ___ ___

YOUNG COW ___ ___ ___

GO FLY A ... ___ ___ ___

TWELVE MONTHS ___ ___ ___ ___

Do you know where President Lincoln was born? Use the clues
to fill in each blank, then read the word in the box to find out.

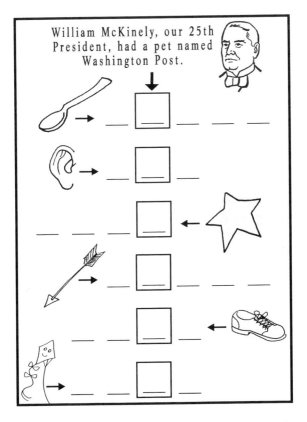

William McKinely, our 25th President, had a pet named Washington Post.

To find out what kind of animal this pet was, use the picture clues to fill in the blanks, then read the word in the box.

This is the only man to serve more than two terms as President of the United States.

BUDGET • SERVE • SMART
TERM • TOUGH • WORK

T	E	G	D	U	B
R	F	R	A	N	K
A	W	E	H	L	I
M	O	V	G	N	D
S	R	R	U	R	O
O	K	E	O	S	E
V	E	S	T	L	T

_ _ _ _ _ _ _ _ _ _ .

_ _ _ _ _ _ _ _

To learn his name, first find these 6 presidential words in the word search. Then write the letters that remain in the order that they appear on the blanks at the bottom of the page.

To find out, follow the path without crossing over any lines. Begin at the arrow.

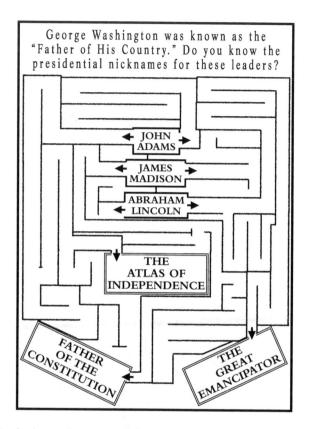

Beginning at the arrows, follow the path from each President's full name, to his nickname.

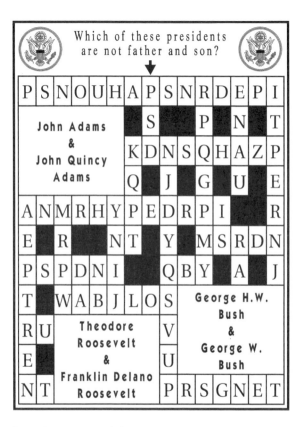

Which of these presidents
are not father and son?

| P | S | N | O | U | H | A | P | S | N | R | D | E | P | I |

John Adams
&
John Quincy
Adams

Theodore
Roosevelt
&
Franklin Delano
Roosevelt

George H.W.
Bush
&
George W.
Bush

Begin at the arrow, and draw a line through the letters as you
spell out the word PRESIDENT. The last letter of the word
PRESIDENT will lead you to the correct pair.

33

All of our presidents had very different
jobs before entering politics.

JOHN ADAMS
WAYER

L _ _ _ _ _

THOMAS JEFFERSON
RCHTCETI

A _ _ _ _ _ _ _ _

ANDREW JOHNSON
AOILR

T _ _ _ _ _

JAMES GARFIELD
EEACHR

T _ _ _ _ _

HERBERT HOOVER
NGIENRE

E _ _ _ _ _ _ _

RONALD REAGAN
RCTO

A _ _ _ _

Unscramble the words to find out each President's occupation.
The first letter of each word has been filled in for you.

34

Beginning at the arrow, travel through this maze without crossing over any lines to find out who said the quote at the top of the page.

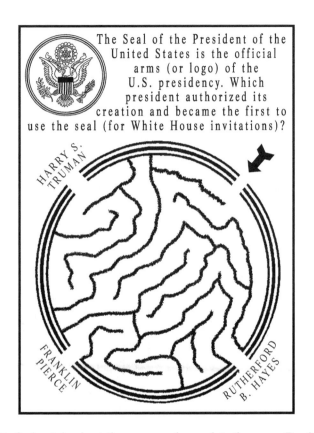

The Seal of the President of the United States is the official arms (or logo) of the U.S. presidency. Which president authorized its creation and became the first to use the seal (for White House invitations)?

HARRY S. TRUMAN

FRANKLIN PIERCE

RUTHERFORD B. HAYES

To find out, begin at the arrow and complete the maze. Don't cross over any lines, and you'll reach the correct name.

Until 1971, both February 12th and 22nd were observed as holidays to honor the birthdays of Abraham Lincoln and George Washington.

___ ___   **1 9 7 1**   ___ ___ ___ ___ ___ ___ ___ ___ ___
J O   Q S F T J E F O U

___ ___ ___ ___ ___ ___ ___   ___ ___ ___ ___ ___
S J D I B S E   O J Y P O

P R O C L A I M E D   O N E
S I N G L E   H O L I D A Y

,

___ ___ ___ ___ ___ ___ ___ ___ ___   ___ ___ ___
Q S F T J E F O U   E B Z

T O   B E   O B S E R V E D
O N   T H E   T H I R D

___ ___ ___ ___ ___ ___   ___ ___
N P O E B Z   P G

F E B R U A R Y ,   H O N O R I N G
A L L   P R E S I D E N T S .

Complete this fun fact by writing the letter of the alphabet that comes **before** each letter on the line above it.

Our 40th U.S. President loved jelly beans. Ronald Reagan kept a jar of them on his desk ... and always picked out his favorite flavor!

Use the picture clues to fill in the blanks. Then read the word in the box to find out President Reagan's favorite flavor.

Which 2 of these U.S. Presidents signed the Declaration of Independence?

GEORGE WASHINGTON

JOHN ADAMS

THOMAS JEFFERSON

JAMES MADISON

Beginning at the arrows, follow each path until you find the two paths that lead to the correct answers.

This U.S. President was born in Honolulu, Hawaii on August 4, 1961. He later served as U.S. Senator from Illinois.

B	A	C	R	A
H	C	K	E	H	U	P
S	S	I	E	I	T	N
O	L	B	A	D
M	A	Y

_ _ _ _ _

_ _ _ _ _ _

_ _ _ _

Cross out every third letter in the puzzle. Write the remaining letters on the line to learn his name.

President John F. Kennedy was a strong supporter of America's young space program when he took office in January 1961. Astronaut Alan Shepard became the very first American in space on May 5, 1961 - only months after Kennedy's inauguration.

total:

How many times can you find the letter **K** hidden in this picture. Write your total on the space provided in the bottom right corner.

Before serving as our 26th U.S. President, Theodore Roosevelt was a soldier. He helped form the First U.S. Volunteer Cavalry Regiment, also known as the "Rough Riders." They became famous during the 1898 Spanish-American War.

Can you find and circle 8 things in picture #2 that make it different from picture #1?

Who was the first president to have a telephone installed in the White House? (This president only did so on a trial basis because so few people had telephones at that time. In fact, the device only called one number: the Treasury Department!)

↳	◁	‡	↓↑	⇋	⇨
A	B	D	E	F	H

↕	▽	↳	▼	⇦	⇧
O	R	S	T	U	Y

"I need to speak with Mr. President!"

▽ ⇦ ▼ ⇨ ↓↑ ▽ ⇋ ↕ ▽ ‡

◁ .   ⇨ ↳ ⇧ ↓↑ ↳

The president's phone number in the White House was simply "1."

Use the decoder above to find the answer. Match each symbol with a letter and then write it on the line.

President Abraham Lincoln was six feet four inches tall. He looked even taller when he wore his stovepipe hat! The top hat did more than just cover Lincoln's head, he kept his important papers in it!

There are seven stovepipe hats hidden in the picture. Find and circle them all.

Which musical instrument did
Harry S. Truman, the 33rd President, play?

BAND
CADENZA
CHORUS
DUET
NOTE
PITCH
SCALE
SING
SONG
STYLE
TEMPO
VERSE

```
D  S  U  R  O  H  C
U  E  S  R  E  V  O
E  L  E  L  A  C  S
T  Y           A  O
E  T           D  N
M  S           E  G
P  I  T  C  H  N  N
O  N  O  T  E  Z  I
P  G  A  D  N  A  B
```

remaining letters:

__ __ __ __ __

unscrambled answer:

__ __ __ __ __

First, find and circle each music word in the word search. Then,
write the remaining letters on the first line, and unscramble
them to find the answer. Write the unscrambled word on the
last line.

45

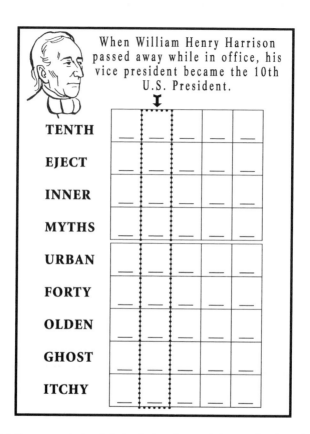

When William Henry Harrison passed away while in office, his vice president became the 10th U.S. President.

TENTH

EJECT

INNER

MYTHS

URBAN

FORTY

OLDEN

GHOST

ITCHY

Put these words in alphabetical order, and then write them in the grid. Read the word in the box to learn the name of the first man to become President by succession.

George Washington, the 1st U.S. President, served two terms. He was the only president inaugurated in two different cities - New York and Philadelphia (as Washington, D.C. had not been created yet).

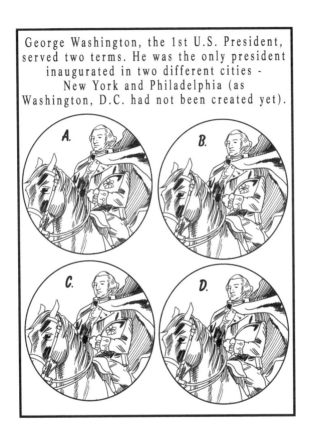

Look carefully at these pictures of George Washington. Can you find and circle the one that is different from the others?

Prior to serving as United States President,
Woodrow Wilson served as president
of Princeton University in New Jersey.

Can you find and circle which one of the five pictures of
Woodrow Wilson is different from all the others?

The president's home at 1600 Pennsylvania Avenue hasn't always been called the "White House." Once officially called the "Executive Mansion," what was the building originally named?

1 B	14 T	7 E	2 H	11 O	4 E
10 P	5 A	9 R	3 S	6 R	12 E
15 N	4 S	8 I	17 T	2 D	1 A
8 E	18 N	4 T	13 I	3 C	20 S
5 U	16 H	22 O	17 S	2 U	1 B
14 S	23 E	19 M	11 O	7 Y	8 E

— — — —

— — — — — — — — — — ,

Circle all the letters that have an **even number** above them. Write the circled letters in the order that they appear on the blank spaces provided to find the answer.

49

During Woodrow Wilson's presidency, a flock of sheep was raised on the White House lawn! The wool was used to raise money for the ongoing World War.

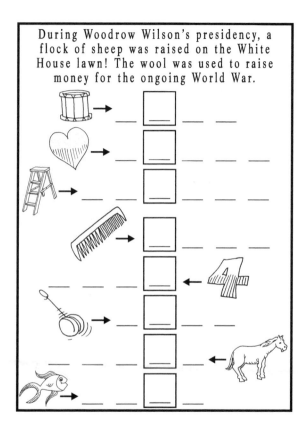

To find out the name of the organization that received the money, use the picture clues to fill in the blanks, then read the word in the box.

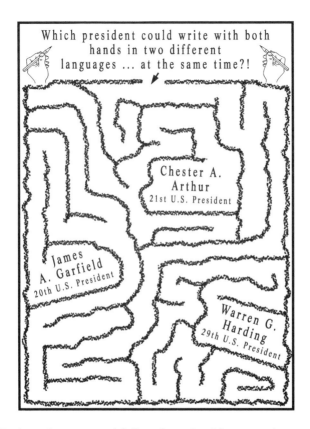

Begin at the arrow and follow the path without crossing over any lines to arrive at the correct answer.

Solutions

Barack H. Obama is our country's first African-American President. Although Obama is the 44th U.S. President, there have actually been just 43. How is that possible?

	1	2	3	4	5	6	7
A	V	N	H	I	T	O	J
B	A	G	F	E	C	I	S
C	L	D	R	W	U	B	K

GROVER CLEVELAND
B2 C6 A2 A6 A1 B4 C3   B5 C1 B4 B4 C1 B1 G2

HELD   OFFICE

TWICE, BUT NOT

IN A ROW. HE WAS
A4 A2   B1   C3 A6 C4   A1 B4   C4 B1 B2

THE   22ND   AND

LATER THE
C1 B1 A3 B4 C3   A5 A3 B4

24TH   PRESIDENT.

Page 4

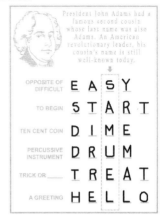

President John Adams had a famous second cousin whose last name was also Adams. An American revolutionary leader, his cousin's name is still well-known today.

OPPOSITE OF DIFFICULT — **E A S Y**

TO BEGIN — **S T A R T**

TEN CENT COIN — **D I M E**

PERCUSSIVE INSTRUMENT — **D R U M**

TRICK OR ____ — **T R E A T**

A GREETING — **H E L L O**

Page 5

Which U.S. territory became a state during Andrew Jackson's presidency (between 1829 - 1837)?

A	W	E	R	D	N	A
J	A	C	K	S	O	N
A	N	D	R	E	W	D
C	D	R		K	E	R
K	R	A		N	R	E
S	E	S	A	S	D	W
O	W	E	R	D	N	A
N	O	S	K	C	A	J

ARKANSAS

Page 6

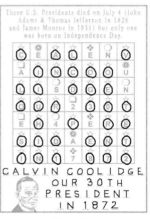

Three U.S. Presidents died on July 4 (John Adams & Thomas Jefferson in 1826 and James Monroe in 1831) but only one was born on Independence Day.

CALVIN COOLIDGE
OUR 30TH
PRESIDENT
IN 1872

Page 7

53

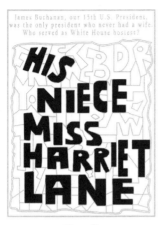

James Buchanan, our 15th U.S. President, was the only president who never had a wife. Who served as White House hostess?

HIS NIECE MISS HARRIET LANE

Page 8

As a Texas businessman who made a fortune drilling for oil before entering politics, 41st U.S. President George H. W. Bush also served as Vice President.

RONALD REAGAN

Page 9

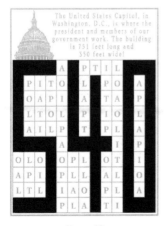

The United States Capitol, in Washington, D.C., is where the president and members of our government work. The building is 751 feet long and 350 feet wide!

Page 10

This president was the first to have a Christmas tree in the White House.

BEFORE	A F T E R	3 1 14 12
FAKE	R E A L	2 11 6
CRUEL	K I N D	5 10 4
CLOSE	O P E N	9 8
ADULT	C H I L D	13 7

FRANKLIN
1 2 3 4 5 6 7 8
PIERCE
9 10 11 12 13 14

Page 11

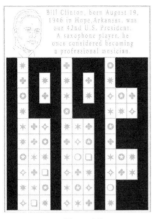

Page 12

Bill Clinton, born August 19, 1946 in Hope, Arkansas, was our 42nd U.S. President. A saxophone player, he once considered becoming a professional musician.

1993

Page 13

Out of the forty men who signed the Constitution of the United States of America, which two went on to become U.S. President?

Benjamin Franklin & Alexander Hamilton

George Washington & James Madison

James Monroe & John Quincy Adams

Page 14

On October 28, 1886 President Grover Cleveland took part in the dedication of a famous American landmark.

STATUE OF LIBERTY

U.S. CAPITOL

LINCOLN MEMORIAL

Page 15

Dwight D. Eisenhower, our 34th President was nicknamed "Ike." Prior to becoming president in 1953, he was a Five Star General during World War Two.

A   B   C   D

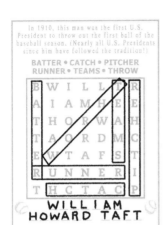

Page 16

In 1910, this man was the first U.S. President to throw out the first ball of the baseball season. (Nearly all U.S. Presidents since him have followed the tradition!)

BATTER • CATCH • PITCHER
RUNNER • TEAMS • THROW

B	W	I	L	L	O	R
A	I	A	M	H	E	E
T	H	O	R	W	A	H
T	A	O	R	D	M	C
E	W	T	A	F	S	T
R	U	N	N	E	R	I
T	H	C	T	A	C	P

WILLIAM
HOWARD TAFT

Page 17

He was the first U.S. President to be born an American citizen. The first 7 U.S. Presidents were born before the U.S. became its own country.

MNAAYLR (Baltimore is its largest city)	MARYLAND
ETSA (The Lone Star State)	TEXAS
SLLINIO (Springfield is the capital)	ILLINOIS
NOVEMT (Leading producer of maple syrup)	VERMONT
RIAAON (The capital city is Phoenix)	ARIZONA
EBNRSAK (Omaha is its largest city)	NEBRASKA
RIUOSIS (The Show-Me State)	MISSOURI
NOROE (Portland is the largest city)	OREGON

MARTIN VAN BUREN

Page 18

Who was the first U.S. President to be born in a hospital?

31ST PRESIDENT
HERBERT HOOVER

36TH PRESIDENT
LYNDON B. JOHNSON

39TH PRESIDENT
JIMMY CARTER

AT THE WISE
CLINIC IN
PLAINS,
GEORGIA

Page 19

He was chosen to replace the vice president in 1973 and later became our nation's leader when the previous president quit - making him the only U.S. President never to run for office.

GLAD	LAD	G
EASY	SAY	E
RENT	TEN	R
HAUNT	HUNT	A
WORLD	WORD	L
DRAW	RAW	D
FOUR	OUR	F
OPEN	PEN	O
RACE	ACE	R
DRINK	RINK	D

56

Page 20

The Founding Fathers of the United States are those who took part in the American Revolution and the birth of our nation. Which U.S. President is credited with coining the phrase "Founding Fathers?"

ADAMS
BRAXTON
FLOYD
FRANKLIN
HALL
HART
JEFFERSON
LEWIS
PACA
PAINE
PENN
READ
ROSS

WARREN G. HARDING

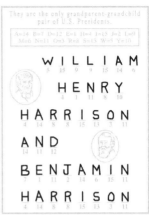

Page 21

They are the only grandparent-grandchild pair of U.S. Presidents.

A=14 B=7 D=12 E=4 H=0 I=15 J=2 L=9
M=6 N=11 O=3 R=8 S=13 W=5 Y=16

WILLIAM
HENRY
HARRISON
AND
BENJAMIN
HARRISON

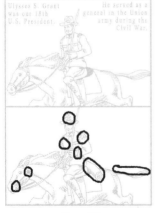

Page 22

Ulysses S. Grant was our 18th U.S. President.

He served as a general in the Union army during the Civil War.

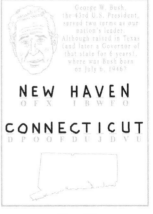

Page 23

George W. Bush, the 43rd U.S. President, served two terms as our nation's leader. Although raised in Texas (and later a Governor of that state for 6 years), where was Bush born on July 6, 1946?

NEW HAVEN
O F X   I B W F O

CONNECTICUT
D P O O F D U J D V U

Page 24

Which annual holiday tradition began during Rutherford B. Hayes' term as our 19th U.S. President?

DISPLAY **SHOW**
HSWO   6 2 12 1

SIP **DRINK**
KNIDR   9 3

DIVIDE **SEPARATE**
SETPARAE   5 8 11   4 7

LARGE **BIG**
GIB   10

WHITE HOUSE
1 2 3 4 5   6

EASTER
7 8   9

EGG ROLL
10   11 12

Page 25

Before serving as president, Andrew Jackson was a colonel during the War of 1812.

Page 26

Although they shared the same last name, these two U.S. Presidents were not related.

Lemon color **YELLOW**
10   9   13

Summer month **AUGUST**
1   16

Day of the week **WEDNESDAY**
0   2 5 8 3

Arc of colors in sky **RAINBOW**
4   11 15 17

Opposite of up **DOWN**
12 7   14

ANDREW JOHNSON &
1 2 3 4 5 6   7   8

LYNDON B. JOHNSON
9 10 11 12 13 14   15   16 17

Page 27

John F. Kennedy, our 35th President, was born on May 29, 1917. This made him the first U.S. President to be born in the

	YES	NO
SHOES ARE WORN ON THE FEET	O	1
DOGS CAN READ BOOKS	3	O
MARBLES ARE SQUARE	H	O
A DIME EQUALS FIVE CENTS	T	O
A BABY CAT IS A KITTEN	O	D
JUNE IS THE SIXTH MONTH	O	A
CARS RUN ON MILK	M	O
BIRDS CAN FLY	O	O
A UNICYCLE HAS FIVE WHEELS	S	O
TEXAS IS A COUNTRY	E	O
SNOW IS COLD	O	S

58

Page 28

Abraham Lincoln, our 16th U.S. President, was the first president born outside of the original thirteen colonies.

QUEEN'S HUSBAND	K I N G	
OPPOSITE OF EAST	W E S T	
FIVE PLUS FOUR	N I N E	
SMALL ROCK	S T O N E	
EIGHT OUNCES	C U P	
YOUNG COW	C A L F	
GO FLY A ...	K I T E	
TWELVE MONTHS	Y E A R	

Page 29

William McKinley, our 25th president, had a pet named Washington Post.

S P O O N
E A R
S T A R
A R R O W
S H O E
K I T E

Page 30

This is the only man to serve more than two terms as President of the United States.

BUDGET • SERVE • SMART
TERM • TOUGH • WORK

T E G D U B
R F R A N K
A W E H L I
M O V G N D
S R R U R O
O K E O S E
V E S T L T

FRANKLIN D.
ROOSEVELT

Page 31

Mount Rushmore is a granite sculpture featuring 4 of our presidents - George Washington, Thomas Jefferson, Theodore Roosevelt, and Abraham Lincoln. Where is it located?

NORTH DAKOTA

SOUTH DAKOTA

MONTANA

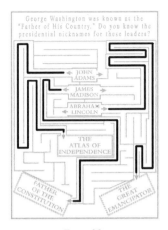

Page 32

George Washington was known as the "Father of His Country." Do you know the presidential nicknames for these leaders?

JOHN ADAMS
JAMES MADISON
ABRAHAM LINCOLN
THE ATLAS OF INDEPENDENCE
FATHER OF THE CONSTITUTION
THE GREAT EMANCIPATOR

Page 33

Which of these presidents are not father and son?

John Adams & John Quincy Adams

George H.W. Bush & George W. Bush

Theodore Roosevelt & Franklin Delano Roosevelt

P S N O U H A G N D E L
S   P   N
K D N S Q H A Z
Q   J G   U
A N M R H Y   D R
E   R   Y   M R D
J   Q B Y   A J
W A B J L O S
U   B
V U
P R S G N E T

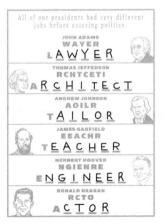

Page 34

All of our presidents had very different jobs before entering politics.

JOHN ADAMS
WAYER
L A W Y E R

THOMAS JEFFERSON
RCHTCETI
A R C H I T E C T

ANDREW JOHNSON
AOILR
T A I L O R

JAMES GARFIELD
EEACHR
T E A C H E R

HERBERT HOOVER
NGIENRE
E N G I N E E R

RONALD REAGAN
RCTO
A C T O R

Page 35

"No president who performs his duties faithfully and conscientiously can have any leisure."

Zachary Taylor
12th President

Millard Fillmore
13th President

James K. Polk
11th President

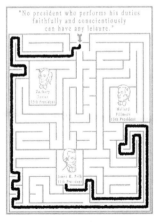

60

The Seal of the President of the United States is the official arms (or logo) of the U.S. presidency. Which president authorized its creation and became the first to use the seal (for White House invitations)?

Page 36

Until 1971, both February 12th and 22nd were observed as holidays to honor the birthdays of Abraham Lincoln and George Washington.

IN 1971 PRESIDENT

RICHARD NIXON

PROCLAIMED ONE SINGLE HOLIDAY

PRESIDENTS DAY

TO BE OBSERVED ON THE THIRD

MONDAY OF

FEBRUARY, HONORING ALL PRESIDENTS.

Page 37

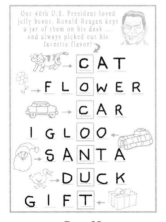

Our 40th U.S. President loved jelly beans. Ronald Reagan kept a jar of them on his desk ... and always picked out his favorite flavor!

CAT
FLOWER
CAR
IGLOO
SANTA
DUCK
GIFT

Page 38

Which 2 of these U.S. Presidents signed the Declaration of Independence?

GEORGE WASHINGTON
JOHN ADAMS
THOMAS JEFFERSON
JAMES MADISON

Page 39

61

Page 40

Page 41

Page 42

Page 43

Page 44

President Abraham Lincoln was six feet four inches tall. He looked even taller when he wore his stovepipe hat! The top hat did more than just cover Lincoln's head, he kept his important papers in it!

Page 45

Which musical instrument did Harry S. Truman, the 33rd President, play?

BAND
CADENZA
CHORUS
DUET
NOTE
PITCH
SING
SCALE
SONG
STYLE
TEMPO
VERSE

scrambled letters:
ONIPA

unscrambled answer:
PIANO

Page 46

When William Henry Harrison passed away while in office, his vice president became the 10th U.S. President.

TENTH
EJECT
INNER
MYTHS
URBAN
FORTY
OLDEN
GHOST
ITCHY

E	J	E	C	T
F	O	R	T	Y
G	H	O	S	T
I	N	N	E	R
I	T	C	H	Y
M	Y	T	H	S
O	L	D	E	N
T	E	N	T	H
U	R	B	A	N

Page 47

George Washington, the 1st U.S. President, served two terms. He was the only president inaugurated in two different cities – New York and Philadelphia (as Washington, D.C. had not been created yet).

63

Prior to serving as United States President, Woodrow Wilson served as president of Princeton University in New Jersey.

Page 48

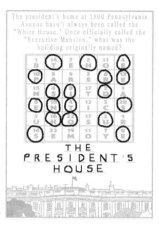

The president's home at 1600 Pennsylvania Avenue hasn't always been called the "White House." Once officially called the "Executive Mansion," what was the building originally named?

THE PRESIDENT'S HOUSE

Page 49

During Woodrow Wilson's presidency, a flock of sheep was raised on the White House lawn! The wool was used to raise money for the ongoing World War.

→ D R U M
→ H E A R T
→ L A D D E R
→ C O M B
F O U R
Y O Y O
H O R S E
F I S H

Page 50

Which president could write with both hands in two different languages ... at the same time?!

Chester A. Arthur
21st U.S. President

James A. Garfield
20th U.S. President

Warren G. Harding
29th U.S. President

Page 51